D0974533

DICK GREGORY

From the Back of the Bus

Edited by Bob Orben
Photographs by Jerry Yulsman

Introduction by
Hugh M. Hefner
Editor-Publisher, *Playboy*

AN AVON BOOK

AVON BOOKS
A division of
The Hearst Corporation
572 Madison Avenue
New York 22, N. Y.

Copyright © 1962
by Dick Gregory Enterprises, Inc.
Published by arrangement
with E. P. Dutton & Co., Inc.
All rights reserved.
Library of Congress
Catalog Card Number: 62-14713
Printed in the U.S.A.

From the
Back of the Bus

This book is dedicated to Abraham Lincoln —
if it wasn't for Abe, I'd still be on the open market.

Dick Gregory

Introduction

DICK GREGORY — comedian, social satirist, Negro, pioneer. In little more than a year he has climbed from $10-a-day car-washer to $5,000-a-week headliner, doing what some said he shouldn't do, most said he couldn't do, but what Gregory knows he must do — telling the truth about segregation so that it brings smiles instead of hurt, and insight, even to the insensitive.

The subject, of course, is still one of tinderbox content — the relationship, real and imagined, between black and white. Dick Gregory has focused the attention of America on its racial problem and has made it laugh, smile, giggle and think. "They almost all realize segregation is wrong," he observes, "but nobody has given them a way out yet. Faces have to be saved."

Many believe Gregory has found the face-saving ingredient — humor. In his gentle, effortless, rambling comment, he kids what has been the unmentionable but with a wit free of the biting edge and the too-sharp point. As a result, his message gets through to the very people he may be cataloguing and, hopefully, takes root.

"People keep telling me some of their best friends are colored. Let's face it. There just aren't that many of us to go round! Personally, I like Negroes. I like them so much, I even had them for parents."

And, sparing no targets: "The N.A.A.C.P. is a wonderful organization. Belong to it myself. But do you realize if tomorrow morning we had complete integration, all them cats would be outta work?"

Facing problems with laughter has been a way of life for Gregory. The second of six children, his first view of the world was from a St. Louis slum. The realization that being a Negro was something apart came soon after. At the age of five he shined shoes for nickels. At first, he wasn't quite sure what the rubbing of his head for "good luck" meant, but the over-tipping roused his suspicions. He stopped shining shoes.

An impoverished family makes a child do strange things. In grammar school the teacher was collecting for the Community

Chest. Each child called out a small amount, and a little girl electrified the group with: "Two dollars!" Dick came next. "Fifteen dollars!" he announced. "My daddy'll give fifteen dollars!" A somewhat questionable pledge, since his family had neither money nor breadwinner, his father having abandoned them some years earlier. The teacher looked at Gregory's face, seeing neither the need nor the pride, and explained: "It's for you and your kind we're taking up this collection." Schools, too, could hurt.

The beacon of hope through these years was his mother, an indomitable woman who met life head on. The electricity was shut off for six months: "Now you know what the dark side of the Moon looks like." Shame at the sight of the relief truck delivering food was met with: "Does everybody get such service?" When the children complained of poverty: "We're broke, not poor. There's a difference."

Gregory, catching hold of this spirit, made it carry him through the rougher stretches of his boyhood. Undernourished and undersized for his age, he found himself a ready target for neighborhood bullies. They teased him about his absent father, the uniform-like relief clothes he wore, until one day Dick had an answer other than tears. He decided to hit first, with jibes instead of jabs, at the very things that hurt most. He laughed at the endless search for jobs, the never-satisfied stomach, the patches and the unpatchable. Gregory was sampling a formula that later was to catapult him into stardom: gather your enemies, your antagonists together and get them laughing! "Once I got them laughing, I could say anything."

He entered high school and concentrated on track. "An education?" He shrugs. "I really didn't care. Went to school in the winter 'cause it was warmer there than it was at home. Remarkable thing about our house. When you came in you never had to knock the snow off your shoes. It wasn't going to melt anyway."

Track, running, the need to leave the past behind him, may have filled some deep emotional cavity within him. His years at Sumner High School found him winning the all-state mile, half-mile and cross-country races. Southern Illinois University offered him an athletic scholarship, and in 1954 he went on to set a college

12

record for the half-mile (1:54.1). But restlessness, an undefined searching for something else, was hard at his heels. He entered the Army.

Special Services became a testing ground for Gregory, and he narrowly missed making the Ed Sullivan Show as a G.I. comic. Eighteen months later he was back at Southern Illinois, pursuing a business administration schedule that held little fascination for him. Shortly before graduation, he packed his bag and headed for Chicago and a job in the Post Office. Almost from the start, it was apparent Gregory had *not* found a home. Frivolity and the U.S. Mail just didn't mix. He insisted the clerks who could sort mail the fastest were the ones who couldn't read and was less than efficient when he dropped letters to Mississippi in the Foreign slot.

Back on the street, he now set his sights on show business as the logical goal. Entering a small neighboring nightclub, he gave the emcee a hard-to-come-by five-dollar bill and went on in his place. Six months of three-nights-a-week, ten-dollars-a-night acceptance followed. Living in a single basement room he wasn't making expenses, but he was making a start. Too soon, the moment of truth arrived. The landlady insisted on rent money past due; Gregory asked for a two-dollar raise and was fired. "I didn't mind being put out of a house; but out of a basement? It was just too ignominious!"

1959 found Dick Gregory in love and in marriage to Lillian, a secretary for the University of Chicago. One year later, their daughter Michelle was born. She came into a family whose net worth and future prospects were every bit as slim as the one her father was born into. Gregory picked up club jobs when he could and supplemented this with such non-comedic chores as car-washing. Christmas, 1960 was a low point — three pounds of hamburger for their holiday dinner, a feast bought with his last dollar bill. "If it weren't for bad luck, I wouldn't have had no luck at all!"

What now? Gregory was certain of the direction he should take. His goal was clubs where the customers "read newspapers." He wanted to shake loose of the blue, single-entendre material so

13

characteristic of small club comics. But would audiences accept anything else from him? The question remained to be answered.

Each day Dick would bundle up little Michelle, sit her in the car beside him and visit booking agents. Lillian had a nine-to-five job, and baby-sitters were a luxury. On one such expedition, the turning point came. The Playboy Club was opening its new Penthouse room and one of the acts, French singer Robert Clary, had been released from his contract at the last minute to go into a Broadway show. We needed a replacement in a hurry and Dick was it. To add to the excitement, the room was honeycombed with Southerners! Dick lit a cigarette and began: "Good evening. It's wonderful to see so many fine Southern people here tonight. I happen to know quite a bit about the South. Spent twenty years there one night."

Warming up to his subject, he drew a fine distinction: "There's only one difference between the North and the South. In the South, they don't care how close I get, as long as I don't get too big. In the North, they don't care how big I get, as long as I don't get too close."

And somewhere near the wind-up, he explained that seemingly disproportionate number of Cadillacs his people own: "They won't let me into your country club so that saves me $500 right there. You *know* I'm not taking my family down to Florida this winter, so there's another $1,500 saved. I walk out of here tonight, get hit by a truck — they ain't taking me to no rich man's hospital. And the city hospital is free, which saves $2,500 more. $500 and $1,500 and $2,500 makes $4,500. General Motors'll sell me anything I want!"

The audience, Chicagoans, Northerners and Southerners, laughed, clapped and begged for more. The original three-week engagement was extended an additional three weeks, and then extended again. And then the second bombshell burst. A young, inexperienced, but inexhaustible press agent, Tim Boxer, badgered a *Time* magazine writer into watching Gregory work. A feature article, "Humor, Integrated," appeared containing such lush praise as: "The audience always laughs and usually applauds the performer, who is just getting started on what may be one of

14

the more significant careers in American show business. With intelligence, sophistication, and none of the black-voice buffoon-ery of Amos 'n Andy, Dick Gregory, 28, has become the first Negro comedian to make his way into the nightclub big time." Dick's rocket was going into orbit.

The rapidity with which he made his climb, after this initial recognition, made for at least one fascinating situation. A few days after the *Time* article appeared, he flew to New York to do the first (of what was to become many) guest shots on the Jack Paar Show. Returning to Chicago the next day, he found his wife in tears: "Three nightclubs and two television producers want you — and our TV set's been repossessed!"

Dick stepped onto the Playboy Club stage for the first time — a complete unknown — and when he stepped down nine weeks later, he was a star and the hottest new act in nightclubdom. All this took place in January and February of 1961, and the course of Gregory's meteoric rise to top salaries, the foremost supper clubs of the nation, feature stories in the leading mass circulation magazines has amazed even show business regulars.

His first record, "Dick Gregory In Living Black And White," was on the best-seller charts for more than half a year. It seemed you couldn't pick up a newspaper without noting the latest Dick Gregory quip. Many of these have become "classics," referred to in editorials and media far beyond the normal scope of nightclub comics.

It would be a rare person in this country who hasn't heard: "I spent six months once, sitting at an Alabama lunch counter. And when they finally served me, they didn't have what I wanted! . . . My brother is so sure he isn't going to get waited on, he don't even take no money with him. . . . Wouldn't it be funny if they finally decided to serve him? If they was ready, and he wasn't?"

But the appeal of Dick Gregory goes far beyond the racial issue. Acutely aware of what is going on in the world, he is an avid reader of newspapers and periodicals. A few minutes before any show he can be seen skimming the latest editions in search of grist for his comedy mill. As a result, his act is as constantly fresh as the daily headlines. Like the best of the new hip comedians, he also improvises, alters and builds his act on stage. Thus, it is a constantly changing, organic thing.

What I like most about my type of humor — it's easy.

Gregory's ability to think fast and funny on the spur of the moment has made him a formidable adversary for hecklers. It takes a courageous person to come back to: "Man, trying to get you to shut up is like trying to explain integration to a lynch mob!" Or: "Don't just sit there and heckle me. Pay your check, burn your cross and leave!" Every now and then, the electric word "nigger" is hurled at him. Gregory's reaction is calm, calculated and effective: "According to my contract, I get fifty dollars from the management every time someone calls me that. Please, do it again. . . . Let's have the whole audience stand up and do it in unison! I'll retire tomorrow!" A crisis is turned into laughter.

Like ripples in a pond, the significance of Dick Gregory is ever-widening. The first comic of his race to gain acceptance in the first-line nightclubs and supper clubs, he has paved the way for others to follow. As one such performer put it: "Greg opened the door. Somebody had to be first. There's room for all of us — he can't work Pittsburgh and Glocca Morra the same night. Negro comedy's untapped. If it doesn't happen for me now, I'll take to driving a truck."

But more than this, Gregory has added a new dimension to the world of comedy. He is a black funnyman who does not get his laughs by fearing ghosts in B movies, rattling "dem bones" or other such demeaning antics. He is another much-needed spokesman for his people, one who can reach the ear of the world in a way that makes it listen. A Jules Feiffer with word pictures — or, as Robert Ruark put it: "The Will Rogers of the Atomic Age" — Dick Gregory is a credit to his, or any, race.

What follows is a sampling of his thought and comment on many different subjects. So picture yourself seated ringside at the posh Playboy Club; the house lights dim; the emcee announces: "Presenting the most talked-about personality in show business today — Dick Gregory, the Negro Mort Sahl!" And Dick Gregory smiles, looks down at the mike base, and observes: "In the Congo, Mort Sahl is known as the White Dick Gregory!"

Hugh M. Hefner,
EDITOR — PUBLISHER,
Playboy

*From
the Back
of the Bus*

Isn't this the most fascinating country in the world? Where else would I have to ride on the back of the bus, have a choice of going to the worst schools, eating in the worst restaurants, living in the worst neighborhoods — and average $5,000 a week just talking about it?

Makes you wonder. When I left St. Louis, I was making five dollars a night. Now I'm getting $5,000 a week — for saying the same things out loud I used to say under my breath.

Are you sure this is the way Martin Luther King got started?

Alabama

Some might say Alabama should come *before* America alphabetically, but not in my book. The way I see it, Alabama is a nice place to visit — but I wouldn't wanna do my act there.

I was thinking of taking a bus tour of Alabama only my Blue Cross has expired. . . . Then again — better *it* than *me!* . . .

Talk about living dangerously, they've got this new game — Freedom-Rider Roulette. You pick from six bus tickets — five go to Chicago and one to Birmingham.

Do you realize the calendar on your wall is called the Gregorian Calendar? You people better be nice to me — or I won't let you use tomorrow.

Apartments

I live in one of those inter-racial apartments. In fact, I was the first one in. They don't care *what* color you are, so long as your money is green. . . . And did we have a ball buying furniture. Up till now, every time we furnished an apartment, we wavered between Swedish Modern and French Traditional — and finally settled on Dime-Store Expendable. . . . But now the sky's the limit. We've even got closed circuit television so you know who's ringing the bell downstairs. Every month you get a thirty-second head start on the rent collector. . . . 'Course, what it really is, is a protective device. We're the only ones who can describe a mugger *before* it happens. . . .

Army

You gotta go some to beat those Army sergeants. I'll never forget the first physical exam they gave me. The sergeant's reading off a list of questions like: "Color?"

I'm no conformist. I said: "Chocolate!" . . . I was gonna add "bitter-sweet" but the psychiatrist was watching. . . .

Then he asks: "Complexion?"

I'm game. I said: "Ruddy!" . . . And after three days of K.P., you know it was? . . .

Then he says: "What were you in civilian life?"

I said: "Deliriously happy!" . . .

I've got nothing against the Army though. I wouldn't even mind fighting to make Berlin and Laos free. Alabama might be next!

Just for laughs, I've been thinking of buying one of those army rocket belts. You saw it in the papers — where you can jump fifteen feet up and land 120 feet away. Gonna take it down to Birmingham and tease Hell outta lynch mobs.

Astronauts

A lot of people have been asking why there are no Negro astronauts. Well I got a surprise for you. One of those seven boys is. He's just looked *this* way since they told him what he volunteered for.

What disturbs me is — all these space trips are going up from the South — from Florida. If I ever go to Mars, I'm gonna have to go through Georgia first. And you *know* which is gonna be more dangerous. . . . Let's face it, Georgia is to the Ku Klux Klan what the Palace was to vaudeville. . . . And this idea of being weightless for hours and hours. We've got little enough weight to throw around in the world as it is. . . .

From left: JOEY BISHOP, DICK GREGORY, EARL WILSON

Brotherhood Week

You remember Brotherhood Week? The only week in the year when you wanna take a Negro to lunch, you gotta ask for a number? . . . I've already got nine invitations to lunch, twelve to dinner, thirty-six to cocktail parties — then come midnight, I turn into a lunch counter again. . . . And you can't turn any of them down, you know. 'Cause Hell hath no fury like a Liberal scorned! . . . If you're on a diet come Brotherhood Week, forget it! . . .

I try to stay away from only one kind of person during Brotherhood Week — the one who believes in integrated washrooms, integrated classrooms, integrated dining rooms — but separated checks. . . . I figure this is my week to make it. Champagne in the fingerbowls — seconds for everybody! Don't invite *me* out unless you *mean* it! . . .

Buses

The more I read — the more I'm convinced — the only bus I'd ever ride through Mississippi is one that offers kitchen privileges. . . . Man, when it comes to rough rides, Teddy Roosevelt's boys had nothing on us! . . .

You just gotta admire those Freedom Riders — going through all that trouble just to eat in a bus stop lunch room. Why it's giving new meaning to those immortal words of Lincoln: "With liberty and heartburn for all!" . . .

I figure, what with cross-country buses, waiting rooms and rest rooms — those Freedom Riders deserve a special kind of award. Like the Order of the Purple Seat! . . .

Can you imagine how it will be, when they hire the first Negro bus driver in the South, and the steering wheel's twenty-five feet long?

Cadillacs

If you really wanna see a classic display of concealed emotion — watch a white insurance adjuster drive up in his Henry J to settle a claim on one of our Cadillacs. . . .

Sometimes I think the only one who doesn't resent us owning a Cadillac is General Motors. . . . This car could be 6,000 skipped lunches standing out at the curb — but you can hear the teeth gritting a block away. . . .

It's kinda hard to describe how we feel about Cadillacs. It's like riding around town in your own bank account. . . . 300 horsepower calling out to the world: "Hello, dere!" . . . GMAC's gift to gracious living. . . . I like it! I like it! . . .

Christmas

All the record stores are playing that subversive song again —
I'm Dreaming of a White Christmas. . . . It's kinda sad, but my
little girl doesn't believe in Santa Claus. She sees that white cat
with the whiskers — and even at two years old, she knows damn
well ain't no white man coming into our neighborhood at midnight. . . . Be honest now. How many of *you* have ever seen a
black Santa Claus? He ain't even black after he comes down the
chimney — and he *should* be! . . .

Once upon a time there was a girl named Little Black Riding Hood.

COURTESY PLAYBOY

Civil War Centennial

Since they started this Civil War Centennial, they're showing a lot of those old movies on TV again. The ones where, at the end, all the slaves are weeping and wailing, cause the South lost. Now ain't that somethin'? That's like Jimmie Hoffa pulling for Bobby Kennedy.

Everybody looks on this Civil War Centennial in a different light. Up in Harlem, all it means is the 100th anniversary of separate rest rooms. . . . That's why the South never suffered from the Recession. Too busy building washrooms. . . .

General Beauregard Gregory   *9:00 A.M., April 9, 1865*

General Ulysses S. Gregory   *7:00 P.M., April 9, 1865*

Color

People keep talking about the white race and the black race—
and it really doesn't make sense. I played Miami last week—met
a fella two shades darker than me—and his name was Ginsberg!
. . . Took my place in two sit-in demonstrations—nobody knew
the difference. . . . Then he tried for a third lunch counter and
blew the whole bit. Asked for blintzes. . . .

Relax, enjoy! You people are backed away from the stage like color was contagious.

Wasn't that nice of them to come up with a Freedom Rider Martini? That's right—a Freedom Rider's Martini. Three and you get stoned!

Wouldn't it be a helluva joke if all this were really burnt cork and you people were being tolerant for nuthin'?

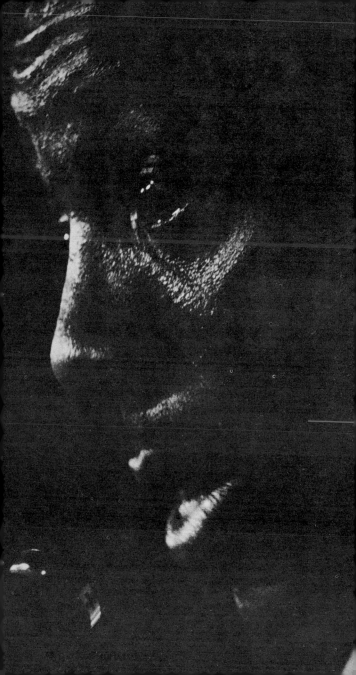

Education

I went to one of those separate but equal schools down South. I don't know how old the textbooks were, but they sure kept me out of the Navy. If people wanted to sail off the edge of the earth — I sure wasn't gonna be one of them! . . . And those Southern history books! Do you realize I was twenty-two before I learned that Lincoln freed the slaves? I always figured Jefferson Davis had us out on probation. . . .

Things were a lot healthier thirty years ago when kids didn't wanna go to school — not because other students were black — or other students were white — but 'cause they didn't wanna go to school.

Kids lead a tough life. Nobody takes them seriously. Nobody listens to them. They're always getting pushed aside. Kids and my people have a lot in common. . . . Only our problems aren't solved by getting older. . . . If man could only get a little older a little later, and a little wiser a little younger.

The good old days! I won't say I'm out of condition now —
but I even puff going downstairs.

Wait a minute, wait a minute, officer....

  You have the nerve to ask me

  how come Negroes do so much cuttin'?

'Cause you don't sell us no damn guns!

Employment

You gotta realize, my people have never known what job security is. For instance, comes another recession and the economy has to tighten its belt — who do you think's gonna be the first notch?

You know why Madison Avenue advertising has never done well in Harlem? We're the only ones who know what it means to *be* Brand X.

I know my wife wondered if she was doing the right thing when I made her give up her job. She still figures the boys in white are gonna get me. Sheets or coats, take your pick.

But the ad said "Engineers." And besides I've no experience as a janitor . . .

I love that expression "survival kit." Up till recently, we used to have survival kits in Mississippi. Ten "Yassuh, bosses" and a shuffle.

Fallout Shelters

What this country needs is a good fifty-dollar combination barbecue pit, swimming pool and fallout shelter — that packs flat for winter, moving or peace.

This international situation raises some interesting ethical problems. Like, if Faubus is driving through one of our neighborhoods when they drop the bomb, would he go into a colored shelter? . . . And if he did — should we let him in? . . . "Orval, stop pounding on that door! Don't you know it's three o'clock in the morning?" . . .

But I'm only kidding. My type of person is the one who builds a fallout shelter with a doorbell.

Fine Point

To me there's no difference in the North and the South. Down South they don't care how close I get as long as I don't get too big; and up North they don't care how big I get, as long as I don't get too close. Yep, we have the same problems up North, 'course up North we're more clever with it. Take my home town, Chicago. When the Negroes move into one large area, and it looks like we might control the votes, they don't say anything to us — they have a slum clearance.

Freedom Rides

You gotta give those Freedom Riders credit. I mean — that takes guts! Anyone who's willing to use the washroom in an Alabama bus station *has* to be some kind of hero. . . .

Do you realize how many people are still in jail from those Freedom Rides? I mean, if you buy a bus ticket for Alabama, and it says GOOD FOR ONE YEAR — you better believe it! . . .

The only reason I wasn't scared is I rode down on one of those new buses with the colored windows, all the mobs looked like friends. My rule is — ride Southern buses in comfort, then get off and run like hell. . . .

Georgia

There is no truth to the rumor that Georgia is passing a law banning mixed drinks.

You all heard of the Ku Klux Klan. That's the Mafia with a drawl. . . . They're having their annual dinner down in Georgia tonight. Formal. Top hat, white sheet and tails. . . .

What do you mean you don't serve U. N. delegates?

H-Bombs

They always talk about Russia dropping *the* bomb. I got news.
If it happens, it's gonna be more like *the 10,000 bombs*. There'll
be a 100-megaton bomb for New York, a fifty-megaton one for
Chicago, a thirty-megaton for Cleveland — and a quarter-megaton
job for Grosse Point (Mich.). And it better be painted white —
'cause if it's black, they ain't gonna let it in! . . . I figure a quarter-
megaton 'cause it doesn't take much for those people to go to
pieces. . . . Like one of us looking at a FOR SALE sign. . . .

I'll say this, we have a nuclear war, and you won't find me
hiding in no fallout shelter. I'm going down to Washington, walk
into each one of those clubs and add my name to the member-
ship roll!

If Red China does produce an atom bomb, they'll be the sixth to do it. There's the United States, Russia, England, France — and the N.A.A.C.P. . . . Oh sure, we've had it three, four years now. Saving it for something really important. Like if the South does rise again — are they gonna have a surprise! . . .

Hecklers

Why you heckling me? You want excitement? Go down to the
N.A.A.C.P. and ask for the white washroom.

You better be nice to me. Chock Full O' Nuts opens forty
more stores — we're gonna be at a premium!

You may be Southern — but you're no Comfort.

No, Madam, I am not the Gregory who was in The Guns of
Navarone.

Now that we've come into a little loot, my wife wants to move to the country. I think she's out of her mind. We could have the only decorator-designed slum in Chicago! . . .

Everything is relative. In Italy there's the Leaning Tower of Pisa, and it's called a wonder of the world. On the South Side we've got buildings leaning just as far—only they're called eyesores. . . . And if you're my color, looking for a house can be quite an experience. Especially when you go to a white neighborhood, offer $40,000 for a $23,000 house, then get turned down 'cause you'd be lowering the realty values. . . .

I'll say this about one of us living in an all-white suburb. Crabgrass *isn't* our biggest problem.

Whaddya mean—

I depreciate your property . . . .

Hypocrisy

Some people have a wonderful way of looking at things. Like the ones who hire one of us to baby sit so they can go to a Ku Klux Klan meeting.

You can respect a person who believes in what he's fighting for. It's the hypocrites who get to you. Like the bartenders who break a glass after you've had a drink — but it isn't your glass — it's a cheaper one — or one that's chipped.

Ku Klux Klan

You know what I don't like? Playing those supper clubs with the white table cloths. On Monday nights, it feels like I'm working a Ku Klux Klan meeting. . . . And for those of you who don't know what the Ku Klux Klan is — that's people who get outta bed in the middle of the night — and take the sheet with 'em! . . .

And I got a surprise for you. You always see pictures of them wearing those pointed hoods? Those hoods are flat! It's the heads that are pointed. . . .

Would you mind holding that burning cross steady? I ran out of matches.

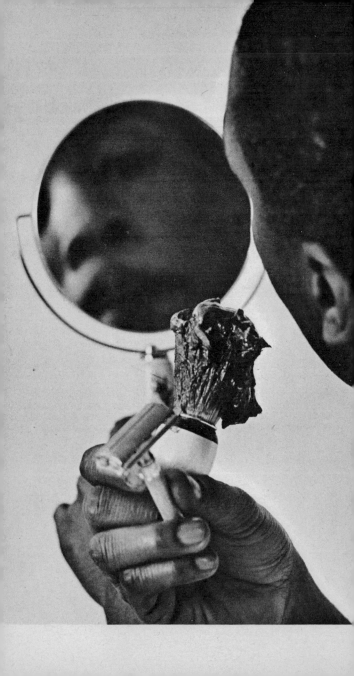

Luck

Me — I'm a born pessimist. The minute I stop looking on the black side of things, I'm out of a job.

I'm sure if I had lived a hundred years ago, with my luck I'd have had the fire insurance concession for Atlanta.

Martin Luther King

Martin Luther has a lot more at stake than the rest of us. If he had to give a report to his Boss tomorrow — how's he gonna explain one year in the pulpit, two years in washrooms, and four in jail? . . . Reverend King's the only celebrity who's given out more fingerprints than autographs. . . .

You think the North has more civil rights than the South, you wake up tomorrow as black as I am and see what happens!

Miami

It's so crowded in Miami, you just don't go down there without reservations anymore. And no one has any more reservations about going to Florida than me.

I'm really kidding. Florida happens to be one of the most liberal states in the South. Why I can go any place I like — restaurants, nightclubs, theaters — and I only have to do one thing. Change my name to Ricardo.

The hotel I stayed at didn't go in for any of this segregation nonsense. Out at the airport, they picked me up, big as life, in a limousine. Even pulled down the shades so I wouldn't get sunburned.

Let's see now. They've broken the four-minute mile; the six-
teen-foot pole vault — how 'bout clearing the color bar next?

New York City

New York is the greatest city in the world — especially for my people. Where else, in this grand and glorious land of ours, can I get on a subway, sit in any part of the train I please, get off at any station above 110th Street, and know I'll be welcome?

Personally, I've always favored New York 'cause this is one city where you don't have to ride in the back of the bus. Not that they're so liberal — it's just that in New York, *nobody* moves to the back of the bus!

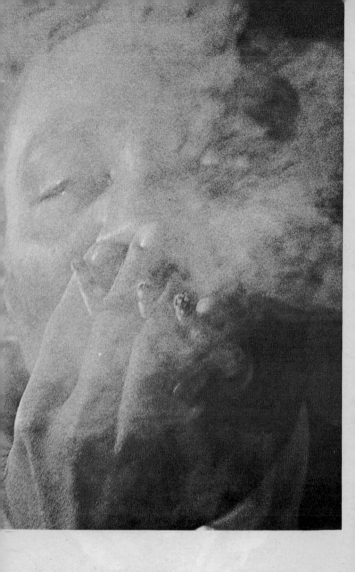

People keep warning me not to smoke so much, but I gotta It's a matter of principle. Like who's running my life — me or the Reader's Digest?

Nudism

I had an uncle who was a practicing nudist down in Georgia —
only no one knew it. Up North, you go around with a few rags
on your back and you're called a sun worshipper. In Georgia,
you're called a tenant farmer. . . . But he had some interesting
ideas on nudism. He felt if everyone took off their clothes,
there'd be no war — cause you couldn't tell your own soldiers
from the enemy. And everybody agreed he had a good idea —
right up to the Congo. . . . I'll tell you one thing about having
naked soldiers. It'd sure make for some wild parades on Decora-
tion Day! . . .

People keep askin' me why they don't send white troops to the
Congo. They should be able to figure it out for themselves —
war brides!

On the Beach

Isn't all this air-conditioning a wonderful thing? Now you can
have more colds in the summer than you do in the winter. . . .

To me summer's come when I get my first invitation to a
wade-in. . . . Wade-in, that's a sit-in with sand in the food. . . .
Bring towels, ear-plugs and bail. . . . But isn't it funny, the more
we get harassed, the more we seem to make of it? Like lynch
mobs. You might ask, what do we have to be thankful to lynch
mobs for? Well, I've got a brother who can run a half-mile faster
than any white boy in the world! . . . Same thing with wade-ins.
They keep pushin' us — Australia better watch out. We already
got one fella swims the hundred yards in fourteen seconds flat.
And carrying a picket sign, that ain't bad! . . .

COURTESY PLAYBOY *From left:* DICK GREGORY, HUGH M. HEFNE

This is where it all started for me. Two years ago, another act got sick, so they put me on instead. Everybody was anxious. They didn't know if I'd start a trend or a riot. . . . I knew I had to make good, cause for all of 1960, I was on sort of an involuntary 900-calorie-a-day program. . . . I was so hungry the first week in this club — the only thing a Bunny meant to me was more meat! . . .

I don't know why they call the Playboy Club a club. It's more like an adult day camp. The magazines always describe the Bunnies as wearing "scanty costumes." Man, on the French Riviera, this'd be considered Brooks Brothers. . . .

But you gotta give Hefner credit. This man doesn't miss a trick. You see those cottontails on the Southern end of the Bunnies? Not only are they cute — but it's impossible to sit down on the job. . . . I also like the subtle way they tell you you're behind in your payments. Put your name up on the wall. . . . I know a dentist who wanted them to add his address and office hours. . . . And if they really wanna get tough, they send a Bunny to your house to ask for the money — while your wife's home. . . .

Look at the size of this crowd! To hell with the show, let's march on Georgia!

Recreation

I have a lot of fun in the summer time. People come up, slap me on the back and I say: "Watch it! My sunburn!" — And you'd be surprised how many apologies I get! . . .

Baseball is very big with my people. It figures. It's the only time we can get to shake a bat at a white man without starting a riot.

And we love to dance — especially that new one called the Civil War Twist. The Northern part of you stands still while the Southern part tries to secede.

But when it comes to recreation, my hat is off to those Roman Emperors who really had the right idea — with those bacchanals and orgies. I mean, group therapy ain't nowhere near it!

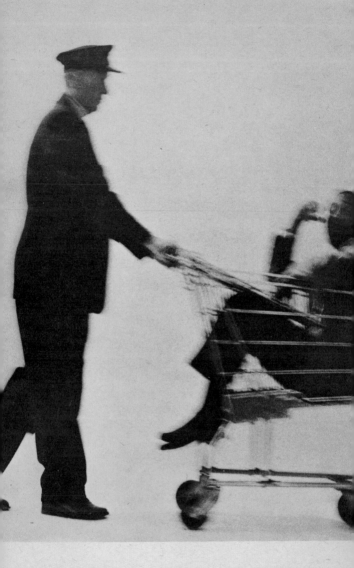

And now, a question for the supermarket managers of America: Where are your shopping carts tonight?

Russia

They claim Russian kids aren't as preoccupied with sex as American teenagers — but don't you believe it. Yesterday they had to expel an abstract physics major — for writing dirty equations.

On some points, I think it's time to stop kidding ourselves. The Russians are ahead of us in a lot of ways — like, you don't see them with a farm surplus problem.

But you gotta admit we're ahead of the Russians in one thing — strikes. . . . I haven't seen so many people walking off their jobs since I asked for a menu in Little Rock. . . .

*Have you ever stopped to think, if all the Negroes left the
South, buses would ride like this?*

St. Patrick's Day

It's so wonderful of all you people to come in wearing green ties and green scarves and shamrocks. How did you know I was Irish? . . . Oh I am! The minute my mother heard the Irish had something called a Free State, we went! . . . And after Alabama, it had to be. . . .

Segregation

So much of this segregation bit is in the mind. People aren't just segregating us. They're segregating themselves too. Like, how many of you have ever tasted hominy grits? Black-eyed peas? Chitlins? No law against it. . . . You try it tomorrow, and I guarantee you won't turn one shade darker. . . . It doesn't make sense — prejudice against foods. I mean, I've been eating gefilte fish for years — even before I knew Sammy Davis, Jr. . . .

You'd be amazed the places segregation pops up in. I went out to the racetrack last week — every horse I bet on was shuffled to the rear.

I don't mind your eating through my act—it's that burping on the punchlines!

Self-Confidence

You gotta say this for the white race — its self-confidence knows no bounds. Who else could go to a small island in the South Pacific where there's no poverty, no crime, no unemployment, no war and no worry — and call it a "primitive society"?

Six of my people have been sitting in the lounge of the best restaurant in town for the last three weeks. Nobody knows if they're sit-ins or if they just haven't tipped the maitre d'.

We're starting a whole new campaign after lunch counters — washing machines! Where else in America are whites and coloreds kept so completely apart? . . . It's like apartheid with a sixteen-pound limit. . . .

Did you know that December 14th is the anniversary of the discovery of the South Pole? I just mention that to show you I'm not prejudiced.

Isn't it fantastic that George Washington Carver found over 300 uses for the lowly peanut — but the South never had any use for George Washington Carver?

I was down in Little Rock last week — which is the only safe position for me to assume in Little Rock. . . . And they won't even allow vanilla-fudge ice cream. Call it Integrated Vanilla. . . . I'm not knocking anybody, you understand — but I'd hate to be the one who sells THINK signs down there. . . .

Are you aware that over 1½ million of my people have left the South since 1950? 1½ million! It's like *Exodus* with pork chops instead of matzohs. . . . And why not? We couldn't get treated any worse down there if we came up with a substitute for cotton. . . . That fine old Southern song says it: Way down South in the land of cotton; where civil rights are soon forgotten. . . .

Southerners

A Southerner is a person who thinks the Sammy Davis Jrs. are just about the nicest couple ever — if it wasn't for him.

I know a Southerner who owned an amusement park and almost went out of his mind — over where to put us on a merry-go-round.

A liberal Southerner is one who'll go to see a performance of GREEN PASTURES, providing it has an all white cast.

They wanted me to volunteer for the space program, but I turned them down. Wouldn't it be wild if I landed on Mars and a cat walked up to me with twenty-seven heads, fifty-nine jaws, nineteen lips, forty-seven legs and said: "I don't want you marrying my daughter neither!"

Man, we're making it. Even the phone company's coming out with colored phones.

Last year I got to stay at the same hotel as the President. Who knows? Maybe next year I'll be a guest at their Virginia estate — riding behind hounds instead of running in front of them.

I was even thinking of dabbling in the stock market, only the broker everybody recommended had a very disturbing word in the name — Lynch!

Today, if a toy manufacturer's gonna make out — he has to come up with something that costs him a dime; lists for ten dollars; sells for $1.98; and needs refills. . . .

Toys also have to be true to life. Like, one of the model railroad companies has come out with the most realistic commuter model yet. Comes with a locomotive, six coaches, and a deficit. . . .

What a ball going through one of those Indian reservations.
Where else could I ever get to be called a paleface?

I was planning to write much more, but prudence dictates we end it here. Governor Faubus may ask for equal space.

If I've said anything to upset you, maybe it's what I'm here for. Lenny Bruce shakes up the puritans, Mort Sahl the Conservatives, and me — almost everybody!

On the other hand, if you've liked the book — don't tell your friends. Just take me to lunch when it's *not* Brotherhood Week.

NOW AVAILABLE
AS AN AVON PAPERBACK

The brilliant, high-spirited, scarring novel by the author of *Native Son*

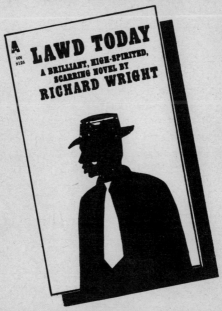

The story of Jake Jackson, a postal clerk in depression-racked Chicago. Jake drinks, gambles, beats his wife and wanders through a one-day odyssey that is completely unforgettable.

"A vivid, harrowing document that rings absolutely true."

—*Chicago Sunday Tribune*

"We come to know not only the society in which Jake lives, but also Jake himself."

—*The Saturday Review*

An Avon Book   **S126**   **60¢**

ANNOUNCING A NEW EDITION
OF A MODERN CLASSIC
JAMES AGEE'S PULITZER
PRIZE WINNING NOVEL

The lyrical and haunting novel that, in the seven short years since its initial publication has become the most beloved and admired book of our time.

An Avon Book   **S133**   **60¢**

We suggest you visit your paperback bookseller for information regarding these outstanding titles. Or, you may write directly to Dept. M, Avon Book Division, The Hearst Corp., 250 W. 55 St., New York 19, N. Y., enclosing the list price of each title plus 10¢ per title to cover the cost of handling and postage.